This book belongs to

_____

Ninja Life Hacks™

Organized Ninja

By Mary Nhin

Pictures by
Jelena Stupar

When Anxious Ninja came over we decided to play a game of checkers.

And, it's like this:

Collections.
Categories.
Checklists.

Collections are so fun! Here's my Lego collection.

I have a lot of different collections. I collect rocks, buttons, and coins.

Another thing I do is use categories.

Categories keep things neat.

When I finish a task, I put a checkmark by it like this!

I was so happy I learned the 3 Cs.

Later that day, we organized my room and the playroom.

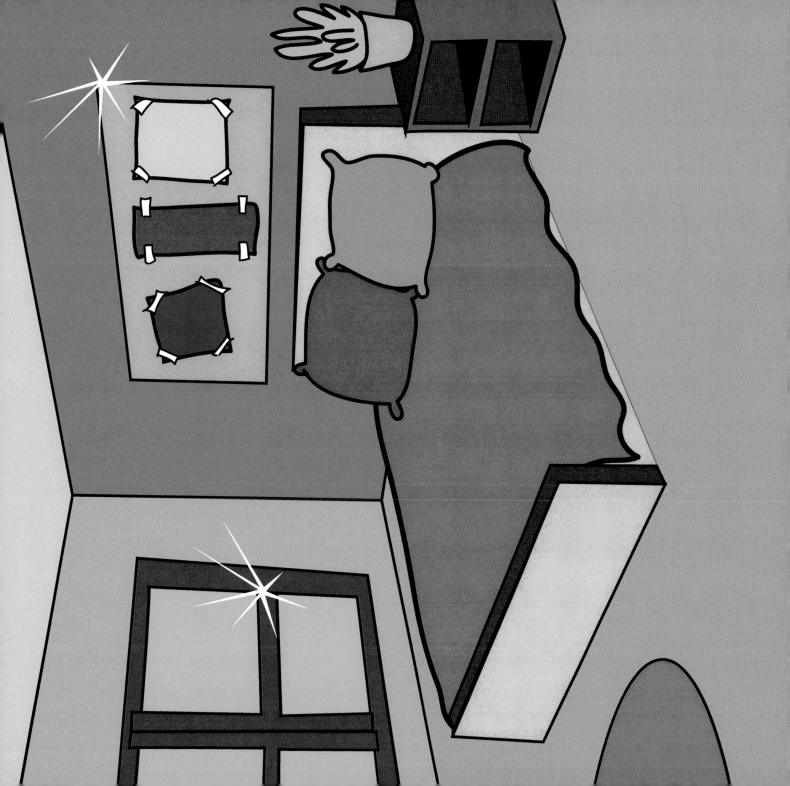

Check out our Ninja Life Hacks Journal, or visit us at NinjaLifeHacks.tv for fun, free printables.

@marynhin @GrowGrit
#NinjaLifeHacks

Mary Nhin Ninja Life Hacks

Ninja Life Hacks

Made in the USA
Monee, IL
28 October 2021